BRYAN LEE O'MALLEY'S

edited by James Lucas Jones | design by Bryan Lee O'Malley & Keith Wood

Published by Fourth Estate

Originally published in 2005 in the United States by Oni Press
www.onipress.com

First published in Great Britain in 2010 by
Fourth Estate
An imprint of HarperCollins*Publishers*
1 London Bridge Street
London SE1 9GF
www.4thestate.co.uk
www.scottpilgrim.com

7

ISBN: 978-0-00-793080-7

Printed and bound by CPI Group (UK)
Ltd, Croydon, CR0 4YY

PRINCIPAL

WHAT ARE YOU IN FOR?

6 The new kid

I GOT IN A FIGHT.

AN AWESOME FIGHT.

DID YOU WIN?

UHHHH... NOT REALLY.

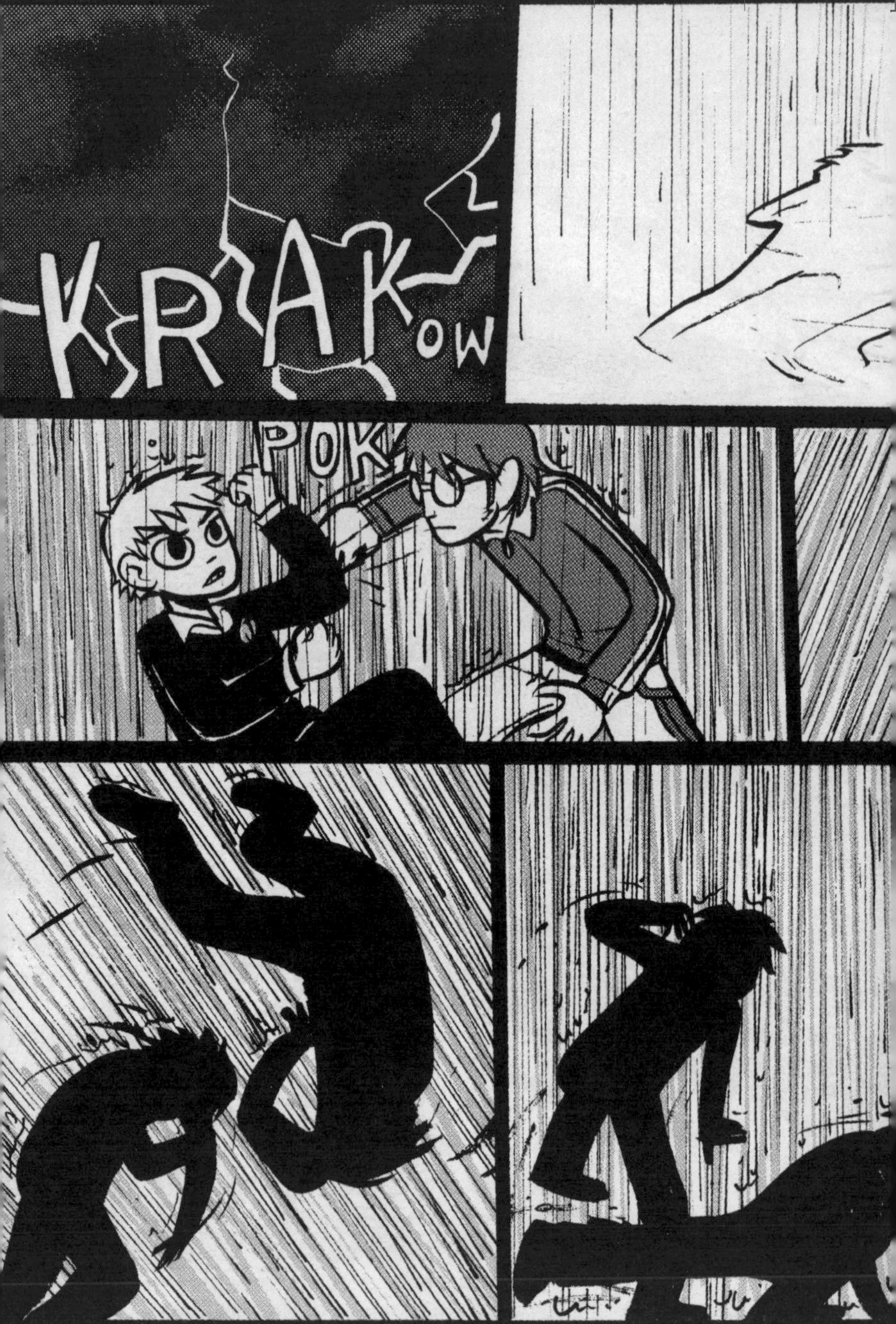
KRAKOW
POK

Dating a High Schooler, Part II

OH, AND I'M HAVING A FRIEND OVER TONIGHT, SO DON'T COME HOME.

WAIT!! WHAT?? WE ARE HOME! THIS IS OUR STOP!

SEE YOU TOMORROW, SCOTT.

YOU SUCK, SURPRISING NO-ONE!!!!

IF BAD WAS A BOOT, YOU'D FIT IT!!!!

YOU'RE A STUPID POO-POO HEAD!

I HAD SEXUAL RELATIONS WITH YOUR MOTHER!!!

YOUR MOTHER HAD THAT COMING HA HA!

YOU, ME AND A MIXTAPE SOON!

I AM ENRAGED AT YOU!

REALLY?

YEAH... UM... I JUST... IT'S NOT GOING TO WORK OUT.

OH...

8

The Late Scott Pilgrim

IT'S ALMOST 11:30, SLACKER! ...AWW, YOU DIDN'T BRING ME ONE?

WHAT, A COFFEE? HOLLIE, I HAVE SOME BAD NEWS. I HATE YOU, OKAY?

YOU HATE *EVERYONE*, KIM.

YOU'RE ONE OF EVERYONE.

HAVE YOU ALWAYS BEEN THIS WAY?

WHAT WAY?

LIKE, UH, A TOTALLY HATEFUL BITCH?

MAYBE I WAS A HAPPY KID.

I CAN'T EVEN IMAGINE.

NO, YOU'RE RIGHT. I WAS LIKE THIS TOTALLY SERIOUS KID, AND THIS TOTALLY ANGSTY TEENAGER.

I PROBABLY ONLY SMILED AND LAUGHED WHEN I WAS DELUDED INTO THINKING IT WOULD MAKE SOME JERK LIKE ME.

YOU'RE A HOLY TERROR, KIM, AND I'M GLAD YOU'RE ON MY SIDE.

DO YOU WANT ME TO PUT A MOVIE ON? I'M GONNA GO GET SOME COFFEE.

OOH, CAN YOU PUT ON SOMETHING REALLY MORBID AND HORRIBLE AND JAPANESE?

SO I HAVE TO *TRAIN*, BY WATCHING THESE MOVIES, AND THEN GO FIND HIM AND FIGHT HIM.

WHAT?!

IT'S A LONG STORY, OKAY?? READ THE BOOK SOMETIME.

ANYWAY, HE'S *EVIL*, AND I HAVE TO FIGHT HIM IF I WANT TO KEEP DATING RAMONA.

OH, YEAH, YOUR *NEW* GIRLFRIEND.

HOW DO YOU KNOW ALL THIS, ANYWAY? ARE YOU ACTUALLY STALKING THE GUY?

WALLACE TOLD ME. WALLACE KNOWS EVERYTHING.

WALLACE WHO?

WALLACE WELLS! MY COOL GAY ROOMMATE?

OH, RIGHT.

HOW'D YOU END UP LIVING WITH THAT GUY, ANYWAY?

I'D RATHER NOT TALK ABOUT IT.

IS IT A REALLY GAY STORY?

THE STORY IS SOMEWHAT GAY, YES.

OKAY,
I'LL HAVE...

HEY!
RAMONA!

COFFEE AGENT

Stacey
Pilgrim

SECOND
CUP

REMEMBER
ME?

HEY,
STACEY!

I DIDN'T
KNOW YOU
WORKED
HERE.

I'M FILLING
IN FOR JULIE
TODAY.
WOW, I
LOVE YOUR
HAIR!

THIS IS *NOT* HOW WE DO IT IN MY *COUNTRY!*

YOUR... HEAD...

SUZETTE!

MIKEY!

THIS IS REALLY BAD.

HE'S KIND OF HOT, THOUGH.

WHAT?

LUCAS LEE? ISN'T HE?

OH, GOD... I THOUGHT *YOU* WERE... *DEAD!*

YOU THINK SO?

COME *ON.* TOTALLY!

HE DIDN'T LOOK LIKE THAT IN HIGH SCHOOL. HE WAS LIKE THIS WHINY LITTLE GREASY-HEADED SKATER.

MAYBE HE'LL GET IT ON WITH THIS CHICK SOON AND WE'LL SEE HIS BUTT.

ANYWAY, KEEP CONVINCING ME YOU'RE NOT GAY, DUDE! YOU'RE DOING GREAT!

H-HEY!

I'M NOT DEAD, MIKEY... BUT YOU ARE!

S... SUZETTE! NO!

HUP!

URK!

YOU'RE COOL, RAMONA. I LIKE YOU.

YOU'RE LAME, BUT I LIKE YOU ANYWAY.

TURN THE MOVIE OFF. ♥

SO HOW ARE YOU, SCOTT? DO YOU HAVE A GIRLFRIEND?

I... UH... KIND OF?

SHE... SHE'S CUTE! YES! STOP ASKING ME ABOUT HER! I'M DONE!

ASK IF SHE'S CUTE!

IS SHE CUTE? DAD WANTS TO KNOW IF SHE'S CUTE.

HOW'S YOUR ROOMMATE? WENDELL? DOES HE HAVE A GIRLFRIEND YET?

N... NO...

HOW ABOUT A JOB? DO YOU HAVE A JOB?

I'M WORKING ON IT! I ALSO DON'T WANT TO TALK ABOUT JOBS! NEXT!

THINGS WILL START LOOKING UP FOR YOU SOON, SCOTT!

WHAT ARE YOU, A FORTUNE COOKIE?

I'M GLAD YOU HAVE A NEW GIRLFRIEND. YOU WERE SO UPSET FOR SO LONG ABOUT N--

YES, I WAS, WASN'T I! GOOD THING *THAT'S* ALL OVER!

DO YOU WANT TO TALK TO DAD?

YEAH! SURE! WHY NOT!

"SCRTCH"

HI SCOTT! DO YOU KNOW WHO THIS IS?

IS IT MY DAD?

YES! HOW DID YOU KNOW?

JUST BE GLAD *YOU* WEREN'T ON THE PHONE!

OH, WHATEVER, PARENTS ARE PARENTS, SUCK IT UP.

YOU KNOW WHERE THEY ARE? THEY'RE IN ROME, THEY'RE LIVIN' IT UP!

THEY'RE... THEY'RE... RIDING VESPAS AND EATING A SPICY MEATBALL AND KISSING PARTS OF THE POPE!

...REALLY?

OR "VENERATING" THEM, OR WHATEVER.

I'M ASSUMING!

DO YOU KNOW ANYTHING AT ALL ABOUT ROME? YOU DON'T, DO YOU?

I DO TOO! I HAVE TONS OF IDEAS ABOUT ROME!

Scott's Ideas About Rome

leaning tower?

a spicy meatball?

the pope of rome?

vespas? are those italian? rome is in italy, right?

gladiator? (this was a movie)

SO LIKE... HOW DID YOU TWO MEET?

UM... IT'S KIND OF COMPLEX.

READ THE BOOK SOMETIME.

THREE! BOIL THE POTATOES 15-20 MINUTES UNTIL TENDER, THEN MASH.

FOUR! HEAT THE OLIVE OIL IN A PAN, ADD THE VEGETABLES AND COOK FOR 15-20 MINUTES UNTIL THEY'RE VERY SOFT. ESPECIALLY THE CARROTS, WHICH ARE PROBABLY THE HARDEST.

UM... I DON'T USUALLY TELL PEOPLE THIS, BUT SCOTT AND I DATED IN HIGH SCHOOL.

WHAT? REALLY?

UH-HUH. IT'S NOT A BIG DEAL OR ANYTHING, BUT...

YOU CAN ADD SOME RED WINE. IT'S AN OPTION. IT MAKES EVERYTHING AWESOME. YOUR OTHER OPTION IS TO DRINK THE RED WINE, WHICH WORKS TOO.

FIVE! ADD THE FAKE MEAT STUFF.

SIX! ADD THE GRAVY STUFF!

EIGHT! ADD SOME SOYMILK AND STIR SO EVERYTHING'S A BIT SAUCY!

THAT'S ALL ANCIENT HISTORY, SO DON'T WORRY ABOUT IT, RAMMY.

RAMMY? ARE YOU SERIOUSLY CALLING HER THAT?

ARE YOU SERIOUSLY CALLING ME THAT?

NO! IT WAS A JOKE! JOKE NAME! HA! HA!

NINE! MASH THE POTATOES WITH SOYMILK AND SOY MARGARINE, MMM, MASHY.

TEN! GET A 9 X 13 BAKING DISH, OR A CASSEROLE OR SOMETHING, AND GLOP THE FAKE MEAT / VEGGIE MIXTURE IN.

ELEVEN! MAKE A LAYER OF POTATOES ON TOP! IN BETWEEN, YOU CAN OPTIONALLY ADD A LAYER OF SLICED TOMATOES, COOKED SPINACH OR CORN.

CHAU RESIDENCE

AWWW... TELL ME ABOUT LUCAS LEE, OKAY? I THINK I'M FIGHTING HIM TOMORROW OR SOMETHING.

WE WERE IN DRAMA CLASS TOGETHER IN FRESHMAN YEAR.

YOU HAD DRAMA CLASS WITH THE FUTURE ACTOR WAS THAT AWESOME?

WELL... WAIT. IT MIGHT HAVE BEEN MATH CLASS. I JUST KNOW I REMEMBER THERE BEING A LOT OF DRAMA.

SO DID YOU HAVE TO FIGHT A LOT OF DUDES?

SCOTT, IT WAS THE NINTH GRADE. HE FOLLOWED ME AROUND. HE WAS A SKINNY LITTLE SNOT-NOSED BRAT.

HE ASKED ME OUT 96 TIMES AND I FINALLY SAID OKAY.

THERE WAS SNOT IN HIS NOSE?

WE WERE FOURTEEN OR WHATEVER. WE WERE KIDS. THERE WAS NO SEX, NO CRIME, NO GREAT HEARTBREAK OR ROMANCE.

WE SAT ON CURBS AND SMOKED.

the next day

UM... HI! LUKE WILSON, RIGHT?

NO, I'M LUCAS LEE.

WHAT IS THIS?

WHO ARE YOU?

ME? I'M SCOTT PILGRIM.

OH, OKAY.

TAP TAP

FLICK

WHAT ABOUT THEM?

WELL, YOU'RE A SKATER, RIGHT? OR YOU USED TO BE?

USED TO BE?? I STILL AM! WHAT'S YOUR POINT?!

CAN YOU SHOW ME A COOL TRICK BEFORE YOU KILL ME?

WHAT, ON THE STAIRS? THERE'S LIKE 200 STEPS AND THE RAILS ARE GARBAGE! IT'S IMPOSSIBLE.

IMPOSSIBLE?

TORONTO REFERENCE LIBRARY

**APPROXIMATELY 82 KM OF SHELVING
CLOSE TO TWO MILLION BOOKS**

**MON-THU, 10:00AM-8:00PM
FRI-SAT, 10:00AM-5:00PM
SUN 1:30PM-5:00PM**
CLOSED SUNDAYS ADJACENT TO PUBLIC HOLIDAYS
ALSO CLOSED SUNDAYS MAY TO THANKSGIVING

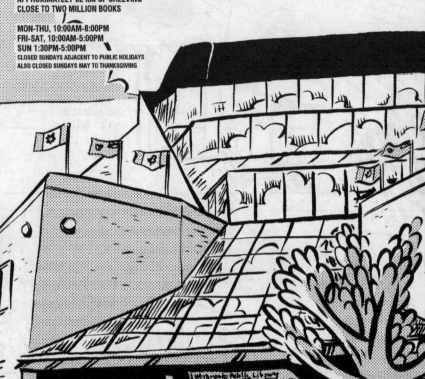

10
Nothing's ever over

KNIVES CHAU
17 YEARS OLD

WHAT?? THEY WENT SOMEWHERE *TOGETHER*?? HOW DOES STACEY KNOW RAMONA?? WHAT THE HELL IS GOING ON WITH THAT?? I TOTALLY FORGOT TO ASK!

I CAN'T BELIEVE YOU WENT AHEAD AND ASKED HER OUT, AFTER I *SPECIFICALLY* TOLD YOU NOT TO DO THAT!

WHAT A *COMPLETE ASS!* IF YOU HURT HER, SO HELP ME, I'LL—

THIS IS SO *MESSED UP!* HOW DO THEY *KNOW* EACH OTHER? AND I TOLD STACEY ABOUT—OH, MAN... I DON'T KNOW ABOUT THIS!

AND FURTHERMORE, MY BEST FRIEND, WHO YOU KNOW AS, MMM, YOUR *EX-GIRLFRIEND*—

WHAT!?

...WELL, SHE'S BACK IN TOWN. AND SHE WAS ASKING FOR YOUR NEW PHONE NUMBER, WHICH I WAS RELUCTANT TO GIVE OUT, FOR THE OBVIOUS REASON THAT YOU'RE A TOTAL JERKWAD, AND—ARE YOU EVEN *LISTENING*??

LA LA LA LA LA LA LA LA LA LA LA LA!

...

THAT
DAY AT THE
LIBRARY...

11

Things Keep Happening

Friday...

SO, YOUR EX-GIRLFRIEND'S BAND.

YEP.

WHAT'S HER NAME AGAIN?

ENVY ADAMS.

REALLY?

WELL, SORT OF. HER INITIALS ARE *N* AND *V*, SO...

ENVY. THAT MAKES SENSE. THAT'S A DECENT BASIS FOR A NICKNAME.

I GUESS, STEPHEN STILLS MADE IT UP, I THINK.

MY INITIALS ARE *R.V.*, SO MY NICKNAME COULD BE TRAILER GIRL. GET IT?

THE V IS FOR VICTORIA.

OH, LIKE THE QUEEN?

OH YEAH, YOU GUYS STILL WORSHIP THE QUEEN OR WHATEVER, DON'T YOU!

UHHH... NOT THE ONE THAT DIED A HUNDRED YEARS AGO, NO.

OOH, GO AHEAD AND POKE FUN AT MY POOR QUEENOLOGY, CANADA BOY.

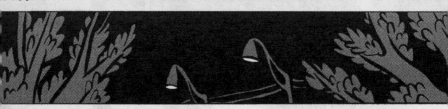

SO, UMMM... DO YOU HATE ME NOW?

WHAT? AM I ACTING LIKE I HATE YOU?

NOT YET...

I DON'T HATE YOU. HEY, TELL ME HOW YOU BROKE UP WITH ENVY ADAMS.

I... WELL, IT'S COMPLICATED.

DON'T YOU WANT TO HEAR ABOUT HOW WE GOT TOGETHER AND EVERYTHING? WE MET AT THE START OF UNIVERSITY--

EWWW! NEW GIRLFRIENDS ONLY WANT TO HEAR BAD STUFF ABOUT EX-GIRL-FRIENDS, DUDE, COME ON.

OH, WELL, WE BROKE UP ON NEW YEAR'S EVE. A YEAR AGO. OVER A YEAR AGO.

WERE YOU WASTED?

NO, I DON'T DRINK.

OH RIGHT.

SO DID SHE GIVE YOU A REASON?

WELL... SHE WANTED TO MOVE TO MONTREAL BECAUSE SHE MISSED HER BEST FRIEND, THIS GUY TODD OR SOMETHING.

AND TWO WEEKS LATER, YOU HEARD THEY WERE SLEEPING TOGETHER, I GUESS?

BASICALLY.

I DATED A TODD ONCE.

GREAT STORY! MAYBE IT WAS THE SAME GUY!

JERK, WHAT'D YOU DO AFTER THAT?

I...

I DON'T REMEMBER.

PUNCH!

BULL!

MY MEMORY OF THAT YEAR IS HAZY. I SWEAR TO GOD, VERY HAZY.

AS IF! DID YOU GRADUATE?

I DON'T REMEMBER.

WHAT EVER!!!

SO AFTER THAT, THE FIRST REAL MEMORY I HAVE IS, THERE WAS THIS RESTAURANT THAT OPENED WAY OUT ON QUEEN WEST—

YOU REMEMBER SOME RESTAURANT BETTER THAN YOUR LAST YEAR OF COLLEGE??

STEPHEN STILLS, YOU GOT A *HAIRCUT?*

YES! SHUT UP!

WHY DON'T I HAVE A HAIRCUT YET? WHY DO *YOU* GET A HAIRCUT?

I WAS NERVOUS! SHUT UP!

DUDE, WE'RE JUST *TALKING* TO HER! IF ANYONE SHOULD BE NERVOUS, IT'S OBVIOUSLY--

I KNOW! SHUT UP!

--OH MY GOD! LOOK AT KIM!

KIM'S WEARING *HIGH HEELS!*

SHE'S VERY, UH... ADAPTABLE.

DID SHE SEDUCE NEIL?

SO YOU DATED HER BRIEFLY?

VERY BRIEFLY!

I BET NEIL WILL DATE HER EVEN BRIEFLY-ER.

I CAN'T BELIEVE THIS!

SHOULD WE TAKE HIM OUT BACK AND BEAT HIM UP?

HEY. I DIDN'T KNOW YOU GUYS WERE COMING TO THIS.

WELL, THEIR FIRST EP WAS OKAY. I HAVEN'T HEARD THE ALBUM YET.

JOSEPH
HER ROOMMATE
24 YEARS OLD

HOLLIE
COWORKER
26 YEARS OLD

HEY, KIM!

BUT THE REAL REASON WE'RE HERE IS BECAUSE JOSEPH HAS A CRUSH ON THEIR BASS PLAYER.

I HAVEN'T SEEN HIM. IS HE HOT?

I DON'T KNOW. IS HE HOT, JOSEPH?

HE IS AS HOT AS THE FLAMES OF THE HELL YOU BITCHES ARE GOING TO.

I WAS IN MONTREAL IN FEBRUARY AND WE HUNG OUT A LITTLE.

HOW DID SHE LOOK?

REALLY GOOD. REEEALLY GOOD.

MONIQUE
OLD CLASSMATE
23 YEARS OLD

SANDRA
SAME DEAL
24 YEARS OLD

DID YOU GIRLS HAVE ANY OTHER CONVERSATIONAL TOPICS IN MIND WHEN YOU CAME OVER TO TALK TO US?

WELL, ARE YOU GOING TO INTRODUCE US?

UHH... THIS IS RAMONA. I THOUGHT YOU KNEW HER.

YEAH, DIDN'T WE MEET AT THAT PARTY THAT ONE TIME?

I GUESS.

SO ARE YOU GUYS AN ITEM NOW?

ARE WE AN ITEM?

I'M SORRY, WHAT?

DUDE.

HI, STEPHEN! I LIKE YOUR HAIRCUT!

OH... UH... HI. THANKS.

I CAN'T WAIT TO SEE THEM PLAY! ARE YOU EXCITED? ARE YOU A BIG FAN?

THEY'RE OKAY...

I CAN'T WAIT TO SEE HER IN PERSON! SHE'S SO COOL.

I HAVEN'T SEEN HER IN A WHILE.

WAIT... WHAT... YOU KNOW HER?

WE... YEAH.

I USED TO BE IN A BAND WITH HER. SHE USED TO DATE SCOTT.

THIS BAND SUCKS.

THAT'S WHAT THEY'LL BE SAYING ABOUT *YOU* ON SUNDAY.

AT LEAST I... WAIT... SOME-THING... YOU... INSULT...

SHIMMY SHIMMY SHIM-MAYYY!

SCOTT, THAT WAS *NOT* A GOOD COMEBACK.

THAT WAS ACTUALLY NOT BAD FOR SCOTT.

HEY, SO I HEAR YOU GUYS ARE OPENING ON SUNDAY TOO...

OH, HEY, YEAH,

SO WE WERE HOPING WE COULD PLAY FIRST, AND YOU GUYS SECOND...

ARE YOU... LUCAS LEE?

NO, I'M LUKE WILSON...

WITH THE GLASSES?

NO. YEAH. WAIT... YEAH.

YOU SEE THAT GIRL?

ISN'T SHE THE DEMONHEADS' DRUMMER?

TOTALLY.

FLIC

OH MY GOD, SHE SMOKES!

OH MY GOD, SHE'S *EVIL!*

PRETTY HOT, THOUGH.

TOTALLY.

and then it was time...

WOO!

I WANT TO GO HOME.

SHH.

and then

dah-malley... — Peacefully, passed away in his 90th year after a brief battle with cancer on Wednesday, January 19, 2005 at Mt. Sinai Hospital. Beloved father of Barbara, cherished grandfather of Stacey and Jennifer, and dear great-grandfather of Stacyanna and Jayden. Brother of Mary Pagon.

Portrait of the author by **Joel MacMillan**

THE AUTHOR'S DETAILS

Bryan Lee O'Malley was born in London, Ontario. His only goal in life was to become rich. At the time of this writing, he is not very rich at all. The *Scott Pilgrim* series is his life's work, after which he plans to retire to a house by the ocean and eat smoked salmon for every meal until his death. He currently lives in an apartment somewhere in Canada with **Hope Larson** and two cats.

www.4thestate.co.uk | *www.scottpilgrim.com* | *www.radiomaru.com*